W9-CEI-826

The Leaves Are Falling One by One

by Steve Metzger
Illustrated by Miriam Sagasti

SCHOLASTIC INC.

New York   Toronto   London   Auckland   Sydney
Mexico City   New Delhi   Hong Kong   Buenos Aires

To Aunt Beverly, Grandma Rose, and Grandpa Louie
— S.M.

To my husband, Leo
— M.S.

Acknowledgements

The author would like to thank Julia Metzger for her creativity and valuable contributions to the writing of this book.

ISBN-13: 978-0-439-02444-0
ISBN-10: 0-439-02444-7

12 11 10 9 8 7 6 5 4 3 2 1   7 8 9 10 11 12/0

Printed in the U.S.A.
First printing, September 2007

The leaves are falling one by one.
Hurrah! Hurrah!
The leaves are falling one by one.
Hurrah! Hurrah!

The leaves are falling one by one.
The red one sparkles in the sun.

And they all go falling down to the ground,
flying in the wind.
Fly! Fly! Fly!

The leaves are falling two by two.
Hurrah! Hurrah!
The leaves are falling two by two.
Hurrah! Hurrah!

The leaves are falling two by two.
Maple leaves land on a young girl's shoe.

And they all go falling down to the ground,
flying in the wind.
Fly! Fly! Fly!

The leaves are falling three by three.
Hurrah! Hurrah!
The leaves are falling three by three.
Hurrah! Hurrah!

The leaves are falling three by three,
fluttering near a bumble bee.

And they all go falling down to the ground,
flying in the wind.
Fly! Fly! Fly!

The leaves are falling four by four.
Hurrah! Hurrah!
The leaves are falling four by four.
Hurrah! Hurrah!

The leaves are falling four by four,
spinning faster, now there's more.
And they all go falling down to the ground,
flying in the wind.
Fly! Fly! Fly!

The leaves are falling five by five.
Hurrah! Hurrah!
The leaves are falling five by five.
Hurrah! Hurrah!

The leaves are falling five by five.
It's fun to watch them swoop and dive.

And they all go falling down to the ground,
flying in the wind.
Fly! Fly! Fly!

The leaves are falling six by six.
Hurrah! Hurrah!
The leaves are falling six by six.
Hurrah! Hurrah!

The leaves are falling six by six,
gliding onto crooked sticks.

And they all go falling down to the ground,
flying in the wind.
Fly! Fly! Fly!

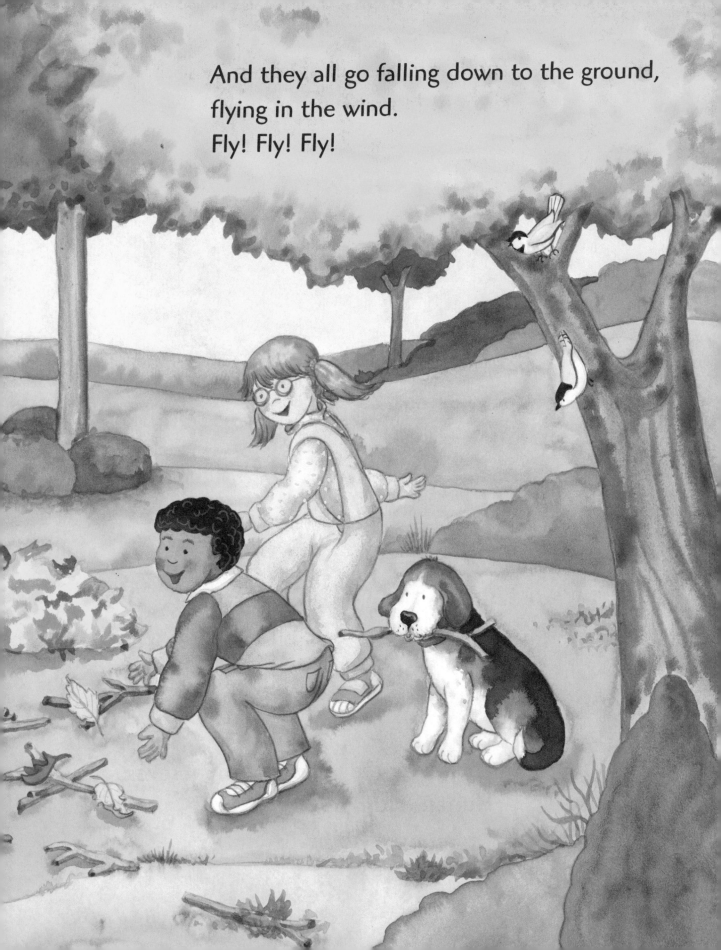

The leaves are falling seven by seven.
Hurrah! Hurrah!

The leaves are falling seven by seven.
Hurrah! Hurrah!

The leaves are falling seven by seven.
Puppy tries his best to get 'em.

And they all go falling down to the ground,
flying in the wind.
Fly! Fly! Fly!

The leaves are falling eight by eight.
Hurrah! Hurrah!
The leaves are falling eight by eight.
Hurrah! Hurrah!

The leaves are falling eight by eight.
Run and catch them — don't be late!

And they all go falling down to the ground,
flying in the wind.
Fly! Fly! Fly!

The leaves are falling nine by nine.
Hurrah! Hurrah!

The leaves are falling nine by nine.
Hurrah! Hurrah!

The leaves are falling nine by nine.
That one's yours and this one's mine.

And they all go falling down to the ground,
flying in the wind.
Fly! Fly! Fly!

The leaves are falling ten by ten.
Hurrah! Hurrah!

The leaves are falling ten by ten.
Hurrah! Hurrah!

The leaves are falling ten by ten.
Here they come again and again.

And they all go falling down to the ground,
flying in the wind.
Fly! Fly! Fly!

Now it's time to jump.
Jump! Jump! Jump!